What they don't tell you about

ANCIENT EGYPTIANS

By David Jay

This book is dedicated to Napoleon,
the mighty French general who went
mad and invaded Egypt. That's when
we started to find out the truth about
the amazing Ancient Egyptians.

Hodder
Children's
Books

a division of Hodder Headline plc

Produced by Lazy Summer Books for Hodder Children's Books

Text by David Jay

Cover portrait BAL 3981 The Gold Mask, Tutankhamun Treasure,
c.1340 BC courtesy of the Egyptian National Museum,
Cairo/Bridgeman Art Libary, London

Published by Hodder Children's Books 1996

10 9 8 7 6 5 4 3 2

ISBN 0340 65614 X

Hodder Children's Books
a division of Hodder Headline plc
338 Euston Road
London NW1 3BH

Printed and bound by Cox & Wyman Ltd, Reading, Berks
A Catalogue record for this book is available from the British Library.

CONTENTS

 Whenever you see this sign in the book it means there are some more details at the FOOT of the page, like here.

RUINS IN THE SAND

Hello, I'm Annie the Archaeologist . I study ancient history – all the bits left behind by people who lived long, long ago. Come with me and I'll tell you all about the weird and wonderful things we've found in Ancient Egypt.

SOLAR TOPEE

PENCIL

NOTEBOOK

DESERT BOOTS

SUNBURNED COMPLEXION

SAFARI SUIT

WATER BOTTLE

BRANDY FOR EMERGENCIES

BRUSH

The Ancient Egyptians were the most amazing and the most mysterious people who ever lived. For thousands of years they built a mighty civilization. Then quite suddenly, the whole thing came to an end.

Archaeologists are people who study the past, mainly by digging up remains from underground.

Many of the beautiful things they had made were stolen by robbers or lay buried for thousands of years. The vast remains of their massive buildings were slowly covered by hot desert sand. Not only that, but the art of reading their strange picture writing was lost, which made the amazing things they left behind seem even more mysterious. Ancient Egypt was one big secret.

WHAT HAPPENED TO THEM?

Ancient Egypt was conquered, first by the Greeks in 332 BC and then by the Romans. The Greeks brought their own language which began to replace Egyptian, and when the Romans became Christian all the beautiful Egyptian temples were shut down, driving out the priests who knew how to read Egyptian writing.

So both the language and the writing died. All that was left were a few scattered objects and buildings-clues to a mystery that no one could solve.

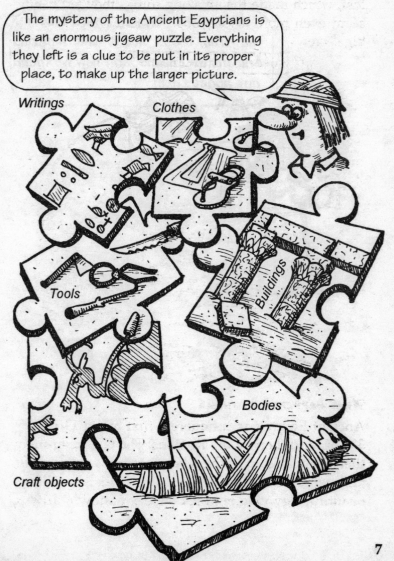

The mystery of the Ancient Egyptians is like an enormous jigsaw puzzle. Everything they left is a clue to be put in its proper place, to make up the larger picture.

Writings

Clothes

Tools

Buildings

Bodies

Craft objects

The search for clues brings us close to the Ancient Egyptians themselves – it's almost as though we can talk to them again, after thousands of years. As we start to solve the mystery we find out that the Ancient Egyptians were even more amazing than the strange things they left behind.

Let's start digging and discover the true facts about the amazing Ancient Egyptians, and how we found out about them.

FANTASTIC
FASHIONS

ANCIENT EGYPT LIVES AGAIN

In 1798 the world-famous French general, Napoleon, landed on the Mediterranean coast of Egypt with an army of 38,000 fierce French soldiers, together with 167 scholars and artists. Napoleon had read the books of eighteenth century scholars about the mysterious remains which travellers brought back from Egypt, and he wanted to find out more about this once-mighty empire.

Actually Napoleon had more urgent reasons for being interested in Egypt...

1. The French wanted to have a new colony.

2. He wanted to cut Britain's links with India, via the Red Sea. France and Britain were at war and India was a British possession.

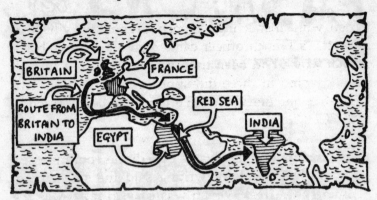

Unfortunately, things went badly wrong for Napoleon. The British, who ruled the seas, soon sank all his ships, and he fled back to France leaving his army and his scholars to their mercy. One good thing came of it however; his scholars began to open up the mysteries of Egypt.

A MESSAGE FROM ROSETTA STONE

The scholars uncovered dusty statues, forgotten temples and beautiful paintings. Many of these long lost remains were covered in writing. But the big problem was – what on earth did all the writing mean?

It looked like a series of pictures, but even the pictures were hard to recognise. No one knew what language had been used or what the picture-characters meant. Translating the writing seemed like an impossible problem.

Then, while inspecting a French fort near the village of Rosetta, a French officer came across a curious black tablet which had been used as part of an old wall. It was covered in three different kinds of writing: two Egyptian and one Greek. The stone had been carved in 196 BC.

The scholars on Napolean's expedition soon guessed that all three kinds of writing said the same thing. Perhaps the Greek, which was easy to read, was the key to unlock the meaning of the Egyptian. They could translate the Greek alright, but they got stuck trying to translate the two kinds of ancient Egyptian.

A young Frenchman, called Champollion, finally cracked the code in 1822. Champollion was a real swot. At thirteen he was studying six ancient languages – Latin, Greek, Hebrew, Arabic, Syriac and

Chaldean! By the age of seventeen he had set his heart on working out the meaning of Egyptian picture writing, or hieroglyphs .

Here's how he did it. It was known that the Egyptians wrote royal names inside a kind of rounded oblong box called a cartouche. In one of these, in the Egyptian writing on the Rosetta stone, was the name Ptolmys (or Ptolemy as we call him now). Champollion was pretty sure of this because the name appeared in the Greek text as well. On another carving he found the name Ptolmys again, and another name which he guessed might be Kleopatra.

P T O L M Y S

K L I O P A D R A

He worked out the four symbols that were common to the two names (l, o, e, t) and then was able to work out the other letters. Using the same method with other words he gradually decoded the Ancient Egyptian alphabet. As a result we have been able to unlock the secrets of the Ancient Egyptians, as written down on papyrus, vellum, wall carvings, paintings and pieces of pottery.

Champion work, Champollion!

'Hieroglyph' means sacred carved writing. It comes from two Greek words meaning sacred and carving.

READ THIS MESSAGE

AND
FIND THE ENTRANCE TO THE PHARAOH'S TOMB

HIEROGLYPHABET

HIEROGLYPH	PICTURE-WORD	SOUND	HIEROGLYPH	PICTURE-WORD	SOUND
	Reed shelter	h		Loaf	t
	Two reeds	y/ee		Water	n
	Foot	b		Reed	i/e
				Water	r

Answer on page 125

Some pairs of letters could sound different in ancient Egyptian.

WALK LIKE AN EGYPTIAN...

The flood of discoveries which followed Napoleon's invasion of Egypt and Champollion's cracking of the code sparked off a wildfire of interest in Ancient Egypt throughout the nineteenth and early twentieth centuries.

1) First came the plunderers

2) Then the serious collectors

3) Then the archaeologists

4) Then the tourists.

Thousands of tons of Egyptian remains were carted off to Europe during the nineteenth century. If you want to see the real thing, you can find cartloads of remains in museums in London, Paris, Berlin, Turin or New York.

By the early twentieth century people were mad about Egyptian styles in clothes and decoration. Egyptian style graced the Titanic, when she slid below the waves in the icy Atlantic. It decorated skyscrapers in New York and was the theme in countless cinemas throughout Europe.

What was it about Ancient Egyptian life-style and fashion that made everyone so excited? Read on...

THE LAND OF THE NILE

A QUICK GUIDE TO ANCIENT EGYPT

The civilisation of Ancient Egypt lasted from about 3100 BC to 330 BC - nearly three thousand years. (This is measured from about the time that the Egyptians began to keep records, but their ancestors had been around for thousands of years before that.)

Most of the time the Ancient Egyptians were ruled by mighty kings, called Pharaohs, who built huge palaces, temples and pyramids along the lush green valley of the Nile. The Pharaohs were thought to be gods as well as kings - that's why the Ancient Egyptians obeyed them. Only Pharaohs could talk to the other gods directly. Ordinary people needed priests, who understood the right prayers, spells and rituals.

The Egyptians were very religious and superstitious. They had gods everywhere – hundreds of small feeble gods and some big important gods like *Osiris*. Osiris was specially important. You see, the Ancient Egyptians were obsessed by a belief in life after death, and when they died, they hoped to be born again in the Egyptian heaven, otherwise known as the *Field of Reeds*, which was where Osiris lived.

The Field of Reeds was a nice place to end up – better than being eaten by a horrible monster, which was the alternative. So it was worthwhile getting ready. No wonder rich Egyptians spent a lot of time and money preparing for death, and no wonder the Pharaohs built huge tombs and pyramids for themselves.

It's lucky for us that they did; much of what we know about Ancient Egypt comes from things which have been found in the tombs of the Pharaohs.

POWER PYRAMID

Once a Pharaoh always a Pharaoh – or a slave, or a smith, or a craftsman for that matter. There was not much movement up or down in Egyptian society; most boys learned their father's trade. A woman's rank was decided largely by who her parents or husband were, and most women worked in the home.

POWER PYRAMID

While Pharaohs and rich scribes left massive tombs and temples behind them, nothing much remains of the ordinary people. Their mud-brick houses have crumbled back into the ground. But we can see how they lived from pictures and writing in the tombs of the rich – and from a few poor objects left buried in the earth.

Most ordinary people were farmers. Their farms grew up along the Nile or by the Fayuum Oasis, a little to the west. The men worked the land and the women worked around the house and raised the children, although sometimes they too worked on the land. Later, as Egyptian civilization became more advanced, men took up public trades or professions outside the home becoming tradesmen, craftsmen, scribes or priests. Some women worked as weavers, laundrywomen or wig-makers, and even more exotic jobs such as priest, dancer or musician. If they were good at wailing, women could become professional mourners.

Without the water of the Nile there can be no farming and so no civilization in Egypt, which would be bone-dry without it. But although the Nile is the life-blood of the country, for hundreds of years no one got round to giving it a name. It was just called "the river".

The Nile was easy to sail; it flowed from south to north while the wind mainly blew from north to south. To go south, you put up a sail. To go north, you took it down.

Small papyrus boats were used on the Nile. Big wooden boats were also used for larger cargoes and for sailing along the coast of the Mediterranean.

People could only live at edge of the delta or on some of the "turtle backs", sandy ridges above the marshes, which the river flowed around.

First Sail Fact

The Nile flowed out into the "Great Green", otherwise known as the Mediterranean Sea. The Egyptians were the first to learn to sail in the Mediterranean.

The river valley of the Nile is from three to fifty kilometres wide, usually no more than twenty, providing a narrow strip of fertile soil. On either side there is desert, which in the early days supported trees and shrubs.

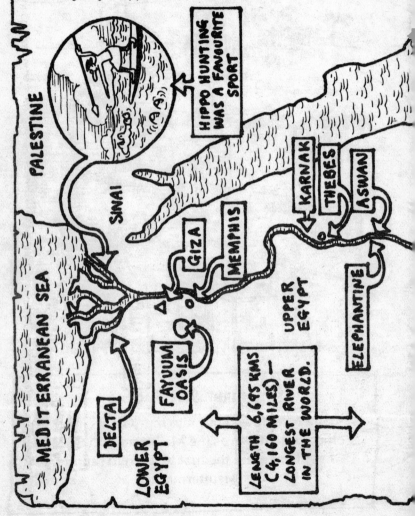

HIPPO HUNTING WAS A FAVOURITE SPORT

PALESTINE

SINAI

KARNAK

THEBES

ASWAN

GIZA

MEMPHIS

MEDITERRANEAN SEA

UPPER EGYPT

ELEPHANTINE

FAYUUM OASIS

DELTA

LOWER EGYPT

LENGTH 6,695 KMS (4,160 MILES) — LONGEST RIVER IN THE WORLD.

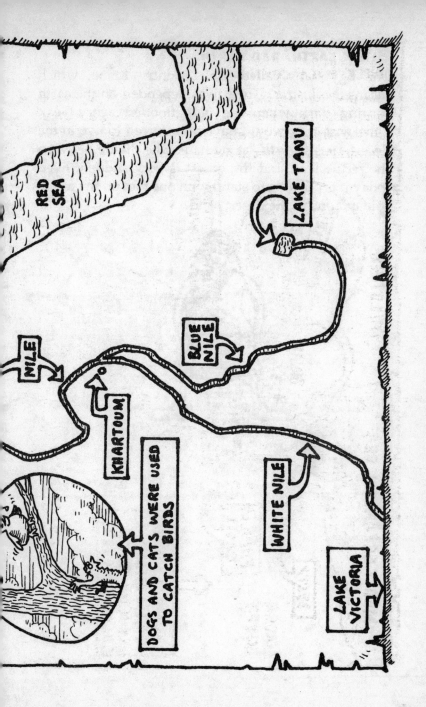

RED SEA

LAKE TANU

NILE

BLUE NILE

KHARTOUM

DOGS AND CATS WERE USED TO CATCH BIRDS

WHITE NILE

LAKE VICTORIA

BLACK EARTH, RED EARTH

The Egyptians called their country Keme, which means *'black earth'*. Their lives depended on the earth turning dark when the Nile flooded every year. Otherwise they would have been forced to live in the desert, or *'red earth'*, as nomads. The divide between the fertile land and the desert is very sudden. Even today it is possible to stand with one foot on the fertile soil and one in the desert sand.

GRAVE BUSINESS

PYRAMIDS AND PYRAMID PILFERERS

The Ancient Egyptians believed so strongly in life after death that they took enormous trouble to make sure that they would be comfortable when they got there. They believed that the soul could not live in heaven unless its physical body was preserved in the form of a mummy on this earth. To protect their mummies in the centuries after they died, they built the most amazing tombs of all time, and filled them with grave-goods to take to the next world.

It was all a waste of time. The first record of a tomb robber dates from 1700 BC, when a robber confessed to taking gold from the tomb of a Pharaoh. (If he hadn't owned up he would have had his nose and ears cut off, or been put to death.) People have been plundering Egyptian graves ever since.

PICK A PYRAMID – HOW PYRAMIDS BEGAN:

A GOOD START

The very first pyramid was the tomb of Djoser. It started off as a mastaba (a flat-top tomb) but was altered six times until it ended up as a *step pyramid*, designed by the architect and Djoser's chief minister, Imhotep . It is still a massive sixty metres high and is the oldest monumental building in the world. Beneath it there are a maze of underground passages.

ONE STEP BACK

At Meidum, there was an attempt to convert a step pyramid into a true pyramid, but they used a softer stone to fill in the steps and the softer material fell away.

SNOFRU PLAYS SAFE

Pharaoh Snofru built a bent pyramid at Dahshur. The angles of the corners start to slope less steeply about half way up. Some say that this was because

GREAT PYRAMID AT GIZA

201 LAYERS OF BLOCKS

BASE AREA 5 HECTARES

SIDES AT BASE 230 METRES

BIG ISN'T IT

BAH!

Imhotep became a god and had special healing powers.

the builders changed their minds after what happened to the pyramid at Meidum.

THE GREAT PYRAMID AT GIZA

The great pyramids are the most massive things ever built, but how they were built remains a mystery to this day. The Ancient Egyptians themselves were
▶ strangely silent about it.

We know that the actual work was done by peasant farmers during the off season when the floods came. It must have been hard work. There was probably a huge workforce which used rollers, sledges, levers, ramps and lubricating oil. All the stone was cut with simple bronze and stone tools.

It seems they built ramps slanting across the sides, going up in a kind of square spiral around the pyramid to the top. There were four of these ramps, one starting at the base of each edge of the pyramid.

HEIGHT 146 METRES

CHAMBER

GRAND GALLERY

QUEEN'S CHAMBER

ENTRANCE

UNDERGROUND

Three were used for taking things up and one for coming down. The core of a pyramid was built first. Then the surface was fixed on, working from the top down.

The Great Pyramid at Giza, built for Pharaoh Khufu during the Old Kingdom, is the most massive building ever. It remained the tallest building in the world for over four thousand years, until the Eiffel Tower was built in 1889.

It was one of the Seven Wonders of the Ancient World and is the only one still standing. When Napoleon saw it and its two neighbouring pyramids, he reckoned there was enough stone to build a wall three metres high around the whole of France.

The geezer who built Giza certainly knew how to run a building site. The Great Pyramid is made up of about 2.6 million blocks of stone, weighing 7 million tons in all. It took twenty-three years to build. It has been worked out that every day about 300 blocks, each weighing about 2.5 tonnes, were put in place. Some stones weighed 15 tonnes. Even if they worked a twelve-hour day, that is a block every about two or three minutes.

This is amazing organisation.

Originally, Giza was covered in a layer of white limestone blocks, which would have looked very bright in the sun, but these were all stolen to help build the city of Cairo, so now it looks sandy. A golden capstone went on top. The blocks of

stone were cut so well, that it was said to be impossible to slide a knife between them.

Inside the Pyramid there were secret passages and chambers to fool thieves. Joining it was a mortuary temple, then a long causeway which led to another temple for the local god, called the cult temple.

No one built pyramids on such a scale again.

FOXING THE ROBBERS

In fact, almost as soon as the Ancient Egyptians started putting things in graves, the graves started being robbed.

Tombs were designed more and more cunningly to outwit the grave robbers. All kinds of tricks, such as false doors, were invented. Guards were hired to protect the tombs, although this wasn't foolproof; in 1100 BC the Mayor of Thebes discovered that the guards themselves were looting the tombs they were meant to protect.

By the time of the New Kingdom, 1560 BC, most pyramids had already been plundered. So the Pharaohs decided to be buried more secretly, in tombs cut out of the rock in a remote valley to the west of Thebes, now called the Valley of the Kings. 62 tombs have been found there. To fool people, they built the temples of the Pharaohs a long way away from the tombs. Pharaohs' wives were buried separately, in the Valley of the Queens.

BOOK OF BURIED PEARLS

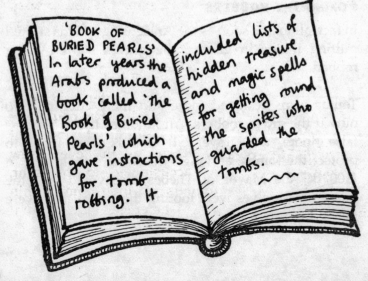

'BOOK OF BURIED PEARLS' In later years the Arabs produced a book called 'the Book of Buried Pearls', which gave instructions for tomb robbing. It included lists of hidden treasure and magic spells for getting round the sprites who guarded the tombs.

Tutankhamen and friends
An amazing find

The boy Pharaoh Tutankhamen was buried in an underground tomb in the Valley of the Kings near Thebes

sometime after 1500 BC. The tomb lay undiscovered for over 3,000 years until a team, led by Englishman Howard Carter and financed by Lord Caernarvon, started to look for it. Carter had noted that there was no record of Tutankhamen's tomb ever having been robbed. He thought it might be complete with all its treasure intact, if they could only find it. He was dead right. Tutankhamen's tomb turned out to be the most amazing find of all time.

In 1922, having worked out where he thought the most likely spot for the tomb might be, Carter began to dig. After only two days, a small boy working with the team found a step beneath the sand. They scraped away the sand and uncovered a doorway, which led to a further inner doorway.

Making a small hole in the inner door, Carter held up a candle. He could see nothing at first, but then "as my eyes grew accustomed to the light, details of the room within emerged slowly from the mist, strange animals, statues and gold - everywhere the glint of gold" - he was peering into a room which was crammed with ancient treasure.

The tomb had been broken into twice before and more than half of the treasure had already been stolen. Even so it was an incredible find. The boy-Pharaoh's body was found inside three coffins nestling one inside the other. The inner one weighed 110 kilograms and was made of 22 carat gold. Its scrap value alone is a million pounds.

The coffins lay inside three stone shrines, the outer one as big as a garage. Tutankhamen's face was covered by a superb mask of gold weighing over ten kilograms. The mummified bodies of two of his still-born daughters were buried with him.

Altogether, Carter spent five years looking for Tutankhamen's tomb, eight years clearing it and ten years listing what he found.

LUGGAGE LIST

Here's a part of what Tutankhamen, the famous boy-king, took with him on his trip to the other world:

DON'T FORGET!

1) 350 litres of oil, two of the jars of oil still with fingerprints on them.

2) 100 items of footwear, made of leather, rushes, wood and gold.

3) Over 150 amulets and other bits of jewellery, which had been placed around his body.

4) 30 kinds of wine, in jars clearly labelled.

5) More than 100 loin cloths.

6) 30 boomerangs.

7) A long trumpet. In 1939 it was blown again for the first time in 3,000 years.

8) A tailor's dummy for modelling his clothes.

9) A first-aid kit.

10) The world's first known sofa bed.

THE CURSE OF OSIRIS

On the day Tutankhamen's tomb was opened, Carter's pet canary was swallowed by a cobra. This innocent bird was the first known victim of a curse which is said to strike all those who open Tutankhamen's tomb. Five months later, Lord Caernarvon also died suddenly. At the moment of his death, the lights went out all over Cairo, and in England his faithful pet terrier howled and dropped dead. Newspapers headlined the "curse of Osiris", and ran stories about the ancient god who ruled in the land of the dead. Carter escaped the curse until he died in 1939.

PHABULOUS PHARAOHS

LORDS OF THE LAND OF SAND

An Egyptian Pharaoh was a really splendid person. He lived like a god. Everyone believed he was a god.

In the beginning Egypt had been divided into two kingdoms, know as Upper and Lower Egypt. Some time after 3000 BC they were united, and from then on the Pharaoh wore a double crown – the white crown of Upper Egypt and the red crown of Lower Egypt. The Pharaoh who united the two Egypts was Menes. He diverted the Nile to create Memphis, the first capital city.

RED CROWN OF LOWER EGYPT

WHITE CROWN OF UPPER EGYPT

DOUBLE CROWN OF THE TWO LANDS

Here's what a Pharaoh needed in his kit:

DOUBLE CROWN

THE GOD HORUS

CROOK

FLAIL

LONG NARROW FALSE BEARD

SCEPTRE

ROYAL RELATIVES TO HOLD POWERFUL POSITIONS

ROYAL FAMILIES

Although women did not often become Pharaohs, the royal line was passed on through both men and women. So Pharaohs tended to marry their sisters or half-sisters or cousins. This custom helped to tie together different branches of a ruling family so that not many members of the royal family got left out.

The Pharaoh usually had a main queen, and perhaps several secondary ones. He also had many concubines. A concubine was like a wife, but of lower social position. All the women lived together in what is now called a harem or women's quarters.

Occasionally there would be a woman Pharaoh. She either ruled on behalf of a weak husband or son, or sometimes grabbed the throne for herself. She needed to have a strong personality to overrule any male contenders.

TO WAR

A Pharaoh's first duties were to make sure that the Nile flooded by using his god-like powers and to defend the country against its enemies. He often chose one of his own sons to be commander-in-chief of the army. Sometimes these royal commanders were only little children.

In actual fact, for long periods of their history the Egyptians lived at peace with the world and rarely had to fight. Egypt was just too far away and too strong to be worth trying to conquer. Later, with improved boat and chariot technology, invasion became easier and there were times when the Pharaohs had to drive off invaders or conquer their neighbours.

AMAZING BATTLE FACTS

 The first
war-horses
may have been
war-donkeys
or asses. Horses
came later.

 Chariots were first brought to Egypt after 1600 BC by the foreign Hyksos . Chariots carried two people, one to drive the chariot and another to fight with spear, sword, axe or bow and arrow. Some clever warriors went solo. They tied the reins round their waist and used both arms for fighting.

Along with the chariot, Egyptians started using armour and the curved sword.

If you were brave in battle, you were awarded a medal called the "Golden Fly".

Dead enemies might have a part of the body cut off, maybe a hand or tongue, so that the winners could count the number of dead.

The Hyksos lived to the east of the Nile delta but probably came from Asia before that.

Check-out these cuttings from my archives!

NILE NEWS

CIRCULATION 3,000,000

Battle first
15th century BC

We are proud to announce in these pages the first ever battle to be recorded in human history, at Megiddo in Palestine, where Pharaoh Tuthmosis III has routed the enemy and is now preparing to lay siege to the town.

Crafty Kadesh foiled by mare's murder
15th century BC

A prince of Kadesh has been foiled in his attempt to outwit our brave troops. Knowing that our Egyptian chariots are pulled by stallions, the prince ordered an especially attractive mare to be released among them. The alluring emissary was killed by our brave soldiers before too many of our best stallions ran off in wild pursuit.

General Djehuty a Basket Case
15th century BC

The port of Joppa has fallen to our brave Egyptian soldiers, due to a crafty trick engineered by General Djehuty. 200 crack troops were smuggled into the besieged city hidden in baskets, breaking free from their hampers inside the walls to open the gates of the city to our main army on the outside. Djust brilliant Djehuty!

Pull the other one, Ram
12th century BC

During an armed clash with the Libyans, Ramses III claims to have killed personally 12,535 of the enemy and to have taken over 1,000 prisoners.

 So many battles were later fought at Megiddo that the Bible uses the name in a different form - Armageddon - to mean a great battle.

Phive Phamous Pharaohs

The best-known Pharaohs ruled in the New Kingdom (1560-1085 BC). Here are five of the most phamous:

Hatshepsut

Hatshepsut started her rule as regent for her nephew and stepson Tuthmosis III. She then made herself "king" of Egypt. She was called "His Majesty" and was always drawn as a man, without breasts and complete with the false beard which all Pharaohs wore.

Among other exploits, she sent her ministers to Punt for myrrh trees and exotic animals to make a zoo, including giraffes and rhinos. In Punt, her ministers found a hugely fat queen. Hatshepsut is the first known horticulturalist and botanist.

Hatshepsut finished her long career by building herself a beautiful mortuary temple. It's still one of the most beautiful buildings in the world.

Tuthmosis III

Hatshepsut's nephew Tuthmosis III came to the throne in his own right when she died. It seems he was so angry at her seizing the throne from him when he was young, that he tried to completely wipe her name out of history. He ordered that her name and picture be scratched out of carvings and drawings. He even pulled down some of her monuments and built a wall around one her obelisks .

Then he started fighting and conquered an empire stretching from Syria to the Sudan. He is said to have had his ears pierced, and to have killed 120 elephants and 120 wild bulls in an hour. Oh yes, and seven lions in a "blink of the eye".

AMENOPHIS III

Tuthmosis' grandson Amenophis III made peace with everyone and settled down to enjoy himself. He liked to live in style:

He once built a lake for a favourite wife. It was over a mile long but took just fifteen days to build.

WHY CAN'T SHE MAKE DO WITH A BATH?

Another of his wives, a foreign princess, brought 317 servant women with her when she moved in.

 An obelisk is a tall needle-shaped monument.

He built two huge seated statues of himself, which still exist, called the Colossi of Memnon. They are 70 metres high and each is carved from a single block of stone brought from quarries over 400 miles away. A crack developed in one of them, and when the wind blew at a certain angle it created a strange singing sound. This amazed several Roman emperors who later visited Thebes.

AKHENATEN

Amenophis III's son, also called Amenophis, was a religious rebel. He changed his name to Akhenaten and moved his capital from Thebes to a new city he had built, called Akhetaten, halfway between Upper and Lower Egypt. He decided that there was only one god, called Aten (meaning the Sun's Disc) and that the other gods didn't exist at all. He closed the temples of all the other gods and ordered the name Amun (the chief of the previous gods) to be hacked off all inscriptions.

Amenophis, or Akhenaten, had wide hips like a woman and big pouting lips. He started a fashion in unisex clothing. One scholar has suggested he was a woman pretending to be man, rather like Queen Hatshepsut only more so. His wife, Nefertiti, was one of the most beautiful women in the world.

After his death all traces of his name were wiped out by the new Pharaoh Tuthankamun, and the city he built was completely forgotten. It was found again by accident in 1887.

RAMSES II

We know about Ramses II because he made sure we would. This was a Pharaoh who really liked to boast. He built huge statues of himself and had his name cut on many monuments built in much earlier times. He reigned for 66 years.

His private life was spectacular. He had eight official wives and over 100 concubines and was said to have fathered over 100 children. He was over 90 when he died, having outlived the first twelve of his sons. The 13th son, Merneptah, was already an old man when he finally became king.

Ramses' mummy was found among 40 others in 1881. X-rays showed that they had packed his nose with peppercorns to keep its hook shape. His mummy had been moved to a crowded tomb, along with several other famous Pharaohs in about 1100 BC to save them from robbers. The coffins were carefully labelled.

Very recently it was noticed that Ramses' mummy was beginning to rot away, so it was sent to a Paris hospital for successful laser treatment on an operating table. Nothing but the best for Ramses.

PHAR OUT PHARAOHS...

THE MADDEST

When Ramses III wanted some myrrh to burn as incense, he decided to send out to the land of Punt to get some. He sent

boats to fetch the myrrh. How did he get the boats to the sea? He had his men pull them across the desert!

THE STRONGEST

Amenhotep II was a Rambo of a Pharaoh. He was famous for his physical strength. None of his soldiers could draw his bow. On one occasion, or so his scribe claims, he drew 300 bows and fired his arrows straight through targets of copper.

44

THE VAINEST

Amenhotep III was pretty vain. He had over 1,000 portraits made of himself.

SPORTING PHARAOHS

Taharqa was a black Nubian Pharaoh. He got his soldiers to trot 30 miles across the desert. Keen on sport, he went along with them – in his chariot. They took just four hours to complete the course.

The oldest sports track in history was around the step pyramid at Saqqara. On the 30th anniversary of a coronation, the Pharaoh was supposed to do a special long-distance jog on the track to prove he was still healthy.

The first ball game seems to have been a kind of cricket. There's a picture of King Tuthmosis with a bat and ball.

Pharaoh Ramses III held the first international sports meeting – a wrestling and quarterstaff contest between Egyptian and enemy soldiers.

A quarterstaff is a long stout stick used for fighting.

THE MOST PHAMOUS

Perhaps the most famous ruler of all was the last - luscious Cleopatra. She was both the wife and the sister of a Pharaoh, whom she soon got rid of. In fact she wasn't a true Egyptian, being descended from a Greek general called Ptolemy.

Cleopatra had a fling with the Roman emperor Julius Caesar and they had a son called Caesarion. Then Caesar was murdered, and she took up with his friend, Mark Anthony, who ruled the eastern Roman Empire. But Octavius, the new leader of the western empire, wasn't happy with Mark Anthony or Cleopatra and he defeated them in a sea battle at Actium off the coast of Greece.

Staring defeat in the face, Anthony and Cleopatra agreed to commit suicide. Antony did it the Roman way, by falling on his sword. Cleopatra hung back and when Anthony was dead, she tried to make friends with Octavius. When Octavious refused her advances Cleopatra finally clasped a poisonous snake, called an asp, to her bosom and gasped her last.

TAKE ME TO YOUR BOSOM

TOP TEMPLES

The Pharaohs may have been gods, but they weren't the most important gods on the block – far from it, Egyptians had loads of gods. There were major gods with huge powers and minor gods with strictly local powers.

HOW IT ALL STARTED – THE BIRTH OF THE GODS

The first god was Re, the sun god . He created two new gods: Nut, the sky goddess, and her brother Geb, the earth god. Geb and Nut had four children, Seth, Osiris, Isis and Nephthys. (You could say that each of them was a bit of a Nut.)

Later a local sun god, Amun, became much more important. Since Egyptians already worshipped Re, the two gods were merged together and called Amun-Re.

Osiris was really good. He brought fertility to the world. His brother Seth was not so good and he was always jealous of Osiris. Seth trapped Osiris in a box and then shoved the box out to sea. Isis, who was fond of her brother Osiris, searched the whole world for him and at last found him stuck in a tree, still in the box. She brought him back secretly to Egypt, but once again the evil Seth struck. This time he tore Osiris' body into 13 pieces and scattered them throughout the country.

Helped by Nephthys, the other sister, Isis, put Osiris back together again and then had a baby by him, called Horus. After Osiris had been torn to pieces and died, he was re-born. This was thought to happen every year when the life-giving Nile flooded, so Osiris was worshipped as the god who kept the world going.

Good God Guide

ANUBIS, GOD OF EMBALMING

HORUS, SON OF OSIRIS, WITH FALCON HEAD. PHARAOHS WERE REBORN VERSIONS OF HORUS

TAWARET, HIPPOPOTAMUS GODDESS OF PREGNANT WOMEN

SOBEK, CROCODILE GOD OF WATER

BAST, CAT MOTHER GODDESS

THOTH, IBIS BIRD GOD OF WISDOM

MAAT, GODDESS OF TRUTH WITH HER FEATHER

THE GREAT TEMPLE

All gods liked to have somewhere to be worshipped. Their temples were mostly quite small, but some were absolutely massive. The remains of the most massive temple of all can still be seen. This is the Great Temple of Amun at Karnak. It was a cult temple.

Cult temples were not for ordinary people but for the priests who served the god. The Great Temple was surrounded by high walls. These vast sloping walls were called pylons and they were crawling with pictures of gods. Outside two huge needles, or

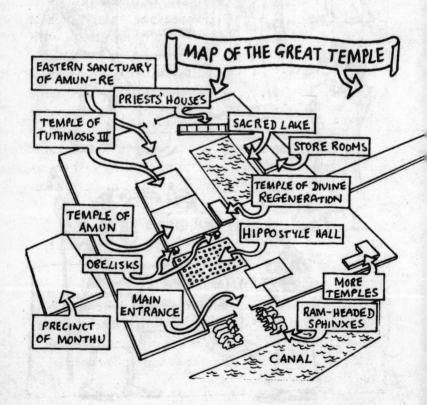

MAP OF THE GREAT TEMPLE

EASTERN SANCTUARY OF AMUN-RE

PRIESTS' HOUSES

TEMPLE OF TUTHMOSIS III

SACRED LAKE

STORE ROOMS

TEMPLE OF DIVINE REGENERATION

TEMPLE OF AMUN

HIPPOSTYLE HALL

OBELISKS

MORE TEMPLES

MAIN ENTRANCE

RAM-HEADED SPHINXES

PRECINCT OF MONTHU

CANAL

obelisks, soared high into the sky. They too were covered in carvings. Inside the walls was the hypostyle hall, its roof supported by 134 pillars, and the inner sanctuary.

The Great Temple was built during the New Kingdom. It was known as "the Most Perfect Place" and covered an area of over a square kilometre (1.5 km by 0.8 km). The Temple was maintained and developed for over 2000 years.

ANOTHER TEMPLE OF AMUN-RE

PRECINCT OF MUT

A large estate spread out around the main building. It housed the many priests and their families, with dormitories, a school, a library, kitchen, granaries, a slaughterhouse, store rooms and farmland. The priests of the cult temples worked as scholars, musicians and farm-labourers, rather as monks did in Christian monasteries.

LUCKY BULL STORY

Ptah, the god who created the world, was very strong and fertile. He was worshipped in the form of a big strong living bull called Apis.

Every now and then the Apis bull would die. Then a great festival was held, and a new bull had to be found. It couldn't be just any old bull. It had to be a big, strong and black with a white patch on its forehead and a white crescent on its neck and sides.

The chosen bull was led to the temple where it was treated like a god-king. It was given servants, loads of food and a harem of cows. From then on until its death it lived a life of ease and luxury. An average Apis bull was reckoned to last 25 years.

Dead Apis bulls were embalmed in a special room. The followers of Apis went into mourning with a strict fast for four days and a less strict fast for 70 days. Then the bull was given a splendid burial just like a Pharaoh.

BUILDING FEATS

Ramses' great temple at Abu Simbel  was positioned so carefully that the sun shone directly into the inner chamber at the spring and autumn equinoxes (halfway between midwinter and midsummer). The sunbeam lit up a statue of the King inside the chamber. A number of the pyramids are lined up with the sun, moon or stars in a similar way. The Ancient Egyptians were brilliant astronomers.

The Great Sphinx is a vast sculpture of a man's head on a lion's body. The face is thought to be a portrait of King Khephren, whose huge pyramid rises beside it. The Sphinx is over 73 metres long and 20 metres high.

In the 1960s the temple of Abu Simbel was moved to higher ground to avoid flooding caused by the new Aswan dam.

Some say the original rock on which the Great Sphinx rests may have first been carved thousands of years before the Sphinx, because of the way the base has been weathered away, as if by rain. By the time the Sphinx was carved there was very little rain in the Sahara, so they say that the original rock and carvings must be much older than anything else in Ancient Egypt.

The largest statue ever to have been cut from a single block of granite was found in Ramses' temple at Thebes.

 Parts of an even bigger statue have been found at Tanis. The big toe is as high as a man's body.

 The first Suez Canal was actually built by Ancient Egyptians in about 600 BC. Traces can still be seen running alongside the modern canal.

SKRIBE SKOOL

> Scribes were the only people who could read, write and calculate. A scribe was bit like a civil servant today. It was a good job and could be a stepping-stone to even better jobs.

GETTING STARTED

To become a scribe, first you had to do well at the scribe school. Only boys of rich families could go to scribe school. Girls and poor people were not allowed and there were no other kinds of schools.

We know what teachers told young would-be scribes because they got their pupils to copy down their advice. They made sure pupils learned what a great thing it was to be a scribe. The teachers liked to encourage their pupils with promises of the great future ahead of them:

> Set your sights on being a scribe; a fine profession. You call for one person and a thousand answer you. You stride freely on the road. You will not be like a hired ox. You are ahead of the others.

But, if this didn't work they took a less gentle approach:

> Do not spend a day of idleness or you shall be beaten. A boy's ear is on his back and he listens when he is beaten.

CAREERS ADVICE

Scribes really liked being scribes. Many tombs proudly show the owner modelled as a scribe, sitting with crossed legs as he writes.

Here's what they did:

- kept records for the Pharaoh
- wrote reports and other documents
- noted down tax returns
- wrote down spells and prayers
- worked as teachers or librarians
- wrote medical or scientific papers

Here's what they needed to do it:

The first pens worked a bit like a brushes. They were made of reed with the top cut so that the reed frayed. Later the stylus became popular. It was a reed with a sharpened point that cut into a coating of wax on papyrus or some other surface.

GET THE PICTURE?

At school scribes were taught picture writing and had to copy out famous writings from the past. They sat in groups writing on flat pieces of pottery or limestone and learned to read by chanting the words.

Here's how their writing developed:

 In the earliest type of writing, pictures meant the things they looked like. To write the word "cat", you just drew a cat.

 Next, they used pictures to show the word's sound, even if the writer had quite a different meaning in mind. This type of writing is called hieroglyphics. If we used hieroglyphics in English, we might write the word *carpet* by drawing a car and then a pet.

Finally, the pictures came to mean simple sounds. So in English for instance, a picture of a cat might have ended up meaning the sound "c".

Actually the Egyptians had three different ways of writing:

1) Simple, clear hieroglyphics or pictures.

2) A squiggled, or *hieratic*, style which was quicker to do.

3) A simple, or *demotic*, style, which was even quicker.

DUCK-FILLED PAPYRUS

In the Nile delta the river is bordered by thick banks of *papyrus* reeds, where ducks, herons and other birds nest. The Egyptians invented a way of turning the reeds into a kind of paper ◄. Here's how they did it:

 Our word "paper" comes from the Latin word "papyrus", the name of the reed that grew by the Nile. Modern paper is made from scraps of fibre, especially cotton and wood, in a method invented by the Chinese in the 2nd century BC.

MAKING PAPER

1) Collect and peel the stalks of the papyrus reed

2) Cut them up into lengths of about 30 cms

3) Slice them lengthwise

4) Lay them out on a cloth side by side and overlapping slightly

5 & 6) Place another layer of strips on top, crossing the first strips at right angles. Then lay another cloth on top.

7) Beat the surface with a mallet until the strips stick together (go on, keep beating!)

8) Put the sticky sheet in the sun to dry

9) Rub it smooth with a stone or hard piece of wood

10) To make a long roll, stick the edges of sheets together with a paste of flour and water

PAPYRUS POINTS

 A scribe, called Amenemope, tried to gather together all existing knowledge, and so invented the world's first encyclopedia in about 1000 BC.

 The oldest book or papyrus in the world is now kept in a Paris museum and dates from about 2000 BC.

 The longest papyrus is now to be found in the British Museum, London. It is 41 metres long.

 The widest papyrus is also in the British Museum. It measures 51 centimetres across.

 Egyptians also wrote on leather, wood and clay. Papyrus took time to make but it was easy to carry in rolls.

 Papyrus reeds were also used to make boats to sail on the Nile.

GIZA JOB

CRAFT CATALOGUE AND OTHER WONDERS

Craftsmen came below scribes in the power pyramid, but they were a cut above the mass of farm labourers. They formed a separate class.

The craftsmen produced so many beautiful objects and paintings that even today there are millions of their products crammed into museums all over the world. It's mainly from these objects that we know what we do about the Ancient Egyptians.

THIS IS A REAL MUSEUM, TRACY, WITH EVERYTHING JUMBLED UP AND INTERESTING

THE INDUSTRIOUS EGYPTIANS

Ornaments were made
of gold, silver and iron.

Carvers carved
pictures out of
stone, called
reliefs,
usually
showing
the
activities
of the
Pharaohs,
other important
people and gods.

Two crafts for women were
weaving and wig-making.

Copper was used to make axes, adzes, knives, daggers, awls, pins, and needles.

Carpenters and cabinet makers made elegant doors, chairs, beds, stools and chests which would be very smart in posh London shops even today.

Potters produced vessels for cooking, eating, drinking and storage. Some of the most beautiful pots the Egyptians ever made were created before writing had been invented.

Weaving was important because the Egyptians loved to dress up in fine linen. They needed linen to dress the dead, too. Wrapping up a dead body could use up 375 square metres of material. Linen was woven from fibres of the flax plant. The best clothes were of incredibly fine cloth, made from the smallest leaves at the top of the plant.

Women did traditional weaving at home and also as a public trade, but when the new, more efficient vertical loom was introduced, weaving became mainly a man's trade.

Here is a description of an Egyptian male weaver:

In his workshop he is in a worse position than the woman in labour. With his knees pushed up against his chest he is unable to breathe the air. If he misses just one day of weaving he is given 50 lashes. He has to bribe the doorkeeper with food to let him see the light of day.

How To Make Linen

1. Pull the whole of the flax plant out of the ground. (The younger the plant, the finer the thread.)

2. Strip the stems into fibres.

3. Spin the fibres and make a ball of thread (the thread twists naturally to the left).

4. Weave into cloth on a loom.

5. Store as rolls or sheets.

6. Store in a dry chest.

SCRIBE JIBES

We know a little bit about working conditions for some jobs from a scribe who was so pleased at being a scribe that he wrote a jokey *Satire of the Trades*, in which he made up lousy job descriptions for those not lucky enough to be scribes like him.

THE SOLDIER

Marches over mountains to Palestine. His bread and water are carried on his back like the load of an ass. His drink is foul water. When he reaches the enemy he is like a pinioned bird and has no strength in his limbs.

THE SMITH

Has fingers like the claws of a crocodile. He stinks more than roe fish.

THE CARPENTER

Wields an adze 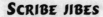. He is wearier than a field labourer. His field is the timber, his hoe the adze. There is no end to his labour.

An adze is a tool for cutting into wood.

THE GARDENER

Carries a yoke which makes his shoulders bend with age; it causes a nasty swelling on his back, which festers. He spends his mornings watering his leeks and his evenings tending to his herbs, having already toiled in the orchard at noon. He works himself into an early grave far more than other skilled men.

THE WASHERMAN

Launders at the riverbank in the vicinity of the crocodile. His food is mixed with filth, and there is no part of him which is clean. He washes the clothes of a menstruating woman. He weeps while he spends all day with a beating stick and a stone.

THE BARBER

Labours until dusk. He travels to a town, sets himself up in his corner, and moves from street to street looking for customers. He strains his arms to fill his stomach, like the bee that eats as it works.

PAY DAY

Life for most workers wasn't as bad as the *Satire of the Trades* made out. People worked four hours in the morning and four in the afternoon, with a break for lunch and a snooze. The working week lasted ten days so there were three weeks in a month, with weekend breaks of two days. On top of this, there were lots of religious holidays.

Most of the time Egyptians had no money or coins. They were paid in kind, for example in linen or beans or onions, and especially in bread and beer. To work out what something was worth, they thought in debens. This was an official weight in copper, although no copper changed hands. A pig was five debens and a goat three. A pair of shoes was two deben and a good coffin was as much as 20.

STRIKE FIRST

The world's first recorded strike happened under
Pharaoh Ramses III. Workmen building his tomb
downed tools because they hadn't been paid.

"We are hungry, 18 days of the month have already
gone by", they complained. "We have no clothes, no
fat, no fish and no vegetables."

TIME FOR CRIME

Policeman seems to be a necessary job in all societies.
Ancient Egypt was no exception. Their methods were
different to nowadays; they used monkeys to arrest
people. They were the first policemen
to use sniffer dogs for tracking
criminals.

Justice was based on a
system of courts.
Anyone could
take a case to
court whether they
were rich or
poor, male or
female. Each case
was decided by a local magistrate. Important cases
were heard by a jury of fellow citizens, and the most
important cases of all by the Pharaoh's chief minister.
Scribes kept a record of trials. Witnesses swore to tell
the truth by Amun, the Sun God, and by the Pharaoh.

WITNESSES COULD BE TORTURED TO MAKE THEM TELL THE TRUTH:

Tortures included beating with a stick, beating on the soles of the feet and the screw  .

A HANDFUL OF HORRID PUNISHMENTS:

For treachery, you might have your tongue cut out. For forgery, you might have your right hand cut off. Noblemen who were found guilty of treason were honour bound to commit suicide.

It all sounds fair enough in its own way. But in fact, although anyone could go to court, the scales of justice were very rusty; the rich were expected to buy their way out of trouble.

 The screw was a torture device, used for crushing bones.

SLOSHED AGAIN!

DOWN ON THE FARM & THE IMPORTANCE OF MUD

Egyptian civilization needed copper, gold, linen, papyrus and a thousand other things. But most of all it needed water and MUD – lovely, thick, black, oozy mud. Both water and mud came with the river Nile.

Once, in Egypt's earliest days, the Sahara had been quite green but now it was largely desert. Sun, water and mud were needed to fight the sands of the desert. The sun was no problem, it was sunny nearly all the time. But there was only a trickle of rain, just a little bit towards the coast. This could have been a big problem - but it wasn't, as long as the Nile kept on flooding. Floods brought water and the sludgy minerals which made things grow.

Because of the floods, growing crops in the Nile Valley was as easy as growing hair. Just scatter seeds and use animals to trample them into the earth. No ploughing, no fertiliser.

When it flooded the water pushed bits of earth and rock beyond the natural banks of the Nile, building up raised bits of land. These then formed walls which held basins of flood water after the flood receded. The floods sloshed everywhere and turned everything into a big lake. In the south, the water level could rise as much as 11 metres. As the water soaked away or evaporated in the sun, it left a rich ooze in which seeds could be planted easily.

At first the country depended on natural floods. Later they learned to control the flow of water over the land so that the water lasted long enough for crops to grow in the season after the floods were over.

WATER WORKS

The volume of water which flooded each year was vital to farmers. It also helped the Pharaohs decide how much to tax them. The higher the floods, the more the farmers could grow and the more the taxman would take. The flood level was the main record kept by the tax-collectors. They measured things in cubits (elbow to finger-tip), palm widths and finger widths. Four fingers made a palm and seven palms made a cubit. Thus the record for a year might say, "Year of the cattle census. The river rose 15 cubits, 2 palms and a finger".

Water was the blood of the country. It was a serious crime to divert someone else's water supply.

THREE WAYS TO MAKE WATER FLOW UPHILL

To make life easier the Egyptians invented ways of lifting water out of the river to irrigate the fields:

The shaduf was a big lever with a weighted pole at one end and a bucket at the other. The weight helped the farmer to lift the bucket. Shadufs can still be seen in modern Egypt.

Archimedes' screw was a giant screw in a tube. As the screw was turned the water climbed up around the thread to the top.

More basically, water was carried in jars hanging from a yoke across the shoulders.

FIRST TIME

Egyptians divided the year neatly into three seasons, all related to the Nile.

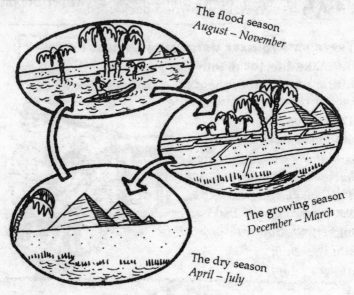

The flood season
August – November

The growing season
December – March

The dry season
April – July

Each season had four months, and each month had 30 days (three weeks of ten days each). Neat so far:

$$3 \times 4 \times 30 = 360$$

Then they threw in an extra five days because they were the first to find out that a year lasts 365 days.

Problem - a year isn't quite 365 days, it's more like 365 days plus an extra quarter day. They didn't allow for the extra quarter. Today, we do this by adding in an extra whole day every fourth (leap) year, but the Egyptians didn't think of that.

So over many centuries, the Egyptian calendar slipped behind. Every 120 years, the calendar slipped by a whole month (120 quarter days = 30 days). Things slowly got completely out of hand. As one of the farmers complained: "Winter is come in summer, and the months come about turned backwards!"

The Egyptians were also the first to divide the day up into twenty-four hours. But the hours weren't always the same! There were twelve hours for daylight and twelve hours for night. So when the days grew longer in summer each daylight hour grew longer and each night-time hour grew shorter!

A SIRIUS START

Egyptians noted that the Dog Star appeared over the horizon just at the beginning of the flood season each year. So this marked the Egyptian New Year, when the long drought was over. Today, we sometimes call this star *Sirius*, a name which comes via the Romans from the name of the Egyptian god *Osiris*.

MUD CAKE

The mud-rich land on either side of the Nile was divided unevenly. The Pharaoh, his relatives, ministers and priests each got huge chunks, and some rich farmers also had large farms. But poor people had tiny farms or just a vegetable patch, so they had to work on other people's land.

The standard crop was wheat, but there were plenty of other things to grow as well:

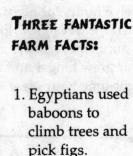

THREE FANTASTIC FARM FACTS:

1. Egyptians used baboons to climb trees and pick figs.

2. Eggs were sometimes hatched by leaving them in warm dunghills.

3. Cows were sometimes force fed with bread balls until they were too fat to walk. This made the meat tender and fatty.

HAPI HARVESTER'S HORTICULTURAL DIARY

Hapi is a farmer and this is his diary.

FLOOD SEASON (AUGUST-NOVEMBER)

Not much farming to do now. May as well take it easy. May stick a few mud patches on the house. Maybe I'll help the wife with her washing and cleaning.

LATER

Oh dear, looks like I shall have to work on that new pyramid they're building for Pharaoh Khufu. Bother! Still at least I don't have to fight in the army.

LATER STILL

Floods going down, back on the farm again. Time to start ploughing with the oxen, then scatter the seeds by hand and tread into the mud with animals.

GROWING SEASON (DECEMBER-MARCH)

Floods falling back. I can see the first seedlings coming up. It's nothing but work, work, work this time of year, I'll have to start weeding soon and check on the channels which bring water to the crops, then there's birds to be scared off by throwing stones at them. It never ends. Better get the wife to scare away the birds.

HARVEST TIME (FEBRUARY TO APRIL)

Today cut wheat with a short sickle hook, tied in sheaves and loaded it into baskets on donkeys. The women brought out a ploughman's lunch (bread and beer and a bit of veg) and then they did flax-pulling and gleaning (collecting bits missed by the reapers). Tomorrow shall take grain taken to the threshing floor, where cattle or goats are driven round and round over it, to separate the grain from the straw, and women toss it in the air to get rid of the light and useless bits of chaff (winnowing). Crops all in late last night, when who puts in an appearance but that nasty taxman? I suppose I'd better offer him a bribe.

COW POWER

Cows were the work-horses, or rather work-cows, of Ancient Egypt. Horses weren't used at all in very early civilizations.

Because cows did all the heavy work, they needed to be looked after. There is a picture of a kindly herdsman offering bread to his ox, which is lying down: "Eat the bread, darling," he says. In another picture a cow is giving birth. "Pull hard, herdsman, she's in pain."

But there were limits to a farmer's kindness. When a hard-working cow grew too old to be useful, she was killed or eaten. Poor people ate every bit from the ears to the feet. The blood was kept for black pudding.

From a cow's point of view, things were worse on some of the big temple estates, where cows were bred purely for their meat. The big temples owned lots of farm animals. One temple kept 834 longhorn cattle, 220 hornless cattle, 2234 goats, 760 donkeys and 974 sheep. Holy cow!

MUMMY!
(THE LIVING
KIND)

GETTING READY FOR BABY

While the men were out in the fields, most women were at home looking after the house and the children – or having them.

They gave birth squatting on a stool, which had a hole in it large enough for a baby to pass through. The mother's stomach was bandaged so that the baby was pushed down inside her body

ARE YOU CALLED SUSAN?

If your name is Susan, you have a very ancient name. It means Lily in ancient Egyptian. It was nearly always mum who named the baby. They could call their babies anything they wanted to. Often they chose animal names like "Frog", "Mouse", "Monkey" or "Hippo". Some names were more unusual. How about "It is our Sister" (pretty obvious that one), or "Blind One", or "I Found her on the West Bank" (this was for a slave). Try this one out for size: "Pediamennebnesttawy" (means gift of Amen, lord of the two lands).

On the whole, families tried to have as many babies as possible. One army captain boasted of having 70 children by one wife!

MILK OR MOUSE?

Egyptians seem to have been loving parents. Babies were breast-fed for three years, which would have helped to protect them against disease. Mothers were advised to test their milk: good milk smelled like dried manna, a type of food, but bad milk had "a stench like fish". Breast milk was often stored in pots and used to help treat couples who couldn't have babies, and to cure burns.

A wet nurse is a woman who breast-feeds someone else's child. They were much in demand, partly because so many women died in childbirth. Wet-nursing could be a bit like farming; an abandoned child might be given to a wet nurse who was paid to raise the child. She might then sell the child into slavery for a profit.

Because babies were breast-fed for such a long time, the babies would have grown teeth before breast-feeding had finished. This could be painful for the wet-nurse or mother. If a baby had teething problems, he or she was given a fried mouse to chew on to help the teeth break through the gums.

KIDS' STUFF

Young children spent most of their time playing naked in the lovely warm Egyptian weather. As they grew older, they were often shaved bald except for the sidelock of youth – a long thick curl at the side of the head, often with a charm attached to the end of it.

When they weren't playing naked in the sun, children dressed and worked just like their parents. Most people started to learn their parents jobs at about seven years of age.

That doesn't mean there was no time to play. Older children could swim in the river, play in fields or model things out of Nile mud. There were lots of toys, like wooden animals, toyboats, wooden balls and spinning tops.

MEETS BOY ♥ GIRL

FROM DATING TO DIVORCE

If a young man or woman wanted to get a girlfriend or boyfriend, it helped to look good. The Egyptians were crazy about looking after their bodies. The whole country seems to have been a bit like Body Shop on Saturday morning.

They used perfumes and two kinds of eyeliner - green or dark grey. Kohl eyeliner, still used by many women today, was originally invented by the Egyptians. As well as making eyes more attractive, kohl helped to protect them against infection. They drew the lines so that their eyes looked larger.

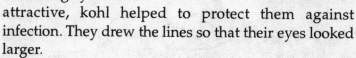

Sometimes they also used lipstick and rouge. Women prepared their make-up in carved toilet palettes and sets.

Tattoos were common in the early years of Egyptian civilization, but later tended to be used only by dancing girls and poorer women, who quite often tattooed a picture of the dwarf-god, Bes, high up on the thigh.

HAIR CARE

In the dusty climate of the Nile, with its lice and other bugs, both men and women tried to remove as much body hair as possible by shaving with razors and plucking with tweezers. They knew that there's nothing a bug likes better than long hair to hide in. Luckily for the bugs, women's hair styles tended to get longer as the years went by. In their long hair they often wore flowers and jewellery.

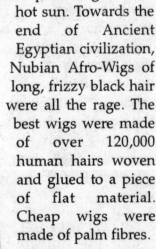

Wigs were popular. They were often worn at dinner parties and could protect against the hot sun. Towards the end of Ancient Egyptian civilization, Nubian Afro-Wigs of long, frizzy black hair were all the rage. The best wigs were made of over 120,000 human hairs woven and glued to a piece of flat material. Cheap wigs were made of palm fibres.

1. To make grey hair dark again: smear it with the blood of a black oxen.

2. To cure baldness: mix fat of lion, fat of hippo, fat of crocodile, fat of cat, fat of snake, and fat of ibex, and spread on head.

3. On the other hand you might want someone to lose their hair. To cure hairiness: spread a mixture of burnt lotus leaf and oil on the head.

WILLOWY WOMEN

In pictures, upper class men are often painted to look fat, but well-off women are nearly always shown looking very, very slim. The slimness is heightened by tight-fitting clothing. Slimness in a woman showed that you hadn't had to develop your muscles with back-breaking work and so was something to show off.

Men wore short skirts, women wore long dresses. These were made of white linen and sometimes embroidered with colours. To contrast with their simple elegant dresses, women often wore collars of red, blue and yellow stones, looking like petals of flowers. They strung beads on their necklaces, belts and girdles. They used shell, bone and ivory to make armlets, bracelets, rings, pendants, lucky charms and combs.

AND FAT WOMEN

In these same pictures the background female workers are painted to look fat, badly dressed, ugly and old. These women are grinding corn, gleaning grain and pulling flax.

LOVE STUFF

The ancient Egyptians loved to love. They showed affection by rubbing noses and kissing. They also wrote love poems and songs:

My heart thought of my love of you when only half my hair was dressed. I came running to find you and neglected my appearance. Now, if you will wait while I plait my hair, I shall be ready for you in a moment.

He is a neighbour who lives near my mother's house, but I cannot go to him. Mother is right to tell him to stop seeing me. It pains my heart to think of him and I am possessed by love for him. True, he's foolish but I'm the same. He doesn't know how much I long to embrace him or he would send word to my mother.

I shall not leave him even if they beat me and I have to spend the day in the swamp. Not even if they chase me to Syria with clubs, or to Nubia with palm ribs, or even to the desert with sticks or to the coast with reeds. I will not listen to their plans for me to give up the man I love.

With her hair she throws lassoes at me, and with her eyes she catches me. With her necklace she entangles me and brands me with her ring.

GETTING MARRIED

Marriage was a simple affair. There wasn't much of a wedding ceremony, apart from a good party in the evening. A marriage usually began when the bride left her father's house to go to her husband's, with all her possessions. Rich people might draw up a marriage contract.

The bride's father would often help the new family with gifts. Sometimes he would go on helping them out for years. Obviously it helped if the husband got on well with his father-in-law.

A man could marry more than one wife, although it was only a rich man who could afford to. There might be many women in a rich household. These would include relatives, maids, administrators and singers as well as wives and concubines.

FAIRLY FREE WOMEN

Egyptian women had more freedom than women of Ancient Greece or Rome. The free behaviour of Egyptian women shocked the Greeks and Romans, who weren't used to it.

Egyptian women could own property in their own right, and when their husbands died they could keep one third of his wealth. So it was a good idea to be nice to your mother or you might not get her money when she died. One older lady said:

FREE WOMAN

I am a free woman of Egypt. I have raised eight children, and have provided them with everything suitable to their station in life. But now I have grown old and behold my children don't look after me any more. I will therefore give my goods to the ones who have taken care of me. I will not give anything to the ones who have neglected me.

SOME MEN LIKED WOMEN...

The scribes of Ancient Egypt were full of good advice:

Found your household and love your wife at home as is fitting. Fill her stomach with food and provide clothes for her back. Make her heart glad, as long as you live.

Do not control your wife in the house when you know she is efficient. Do not say to her "Where is it? Get it" when she has put something in the correct place. Let your eye watch in silence. Then you will see her skill, and it will be a joy when your hand is with her.

SOME MEN DIDN'T LIKE WOMEN...

Here's what one miserable old scribe called Ankhsheshonq had to say about women:

> Instructing a woman is like holding a sack of sand whose sides have been split open.
>
> The idiot who looks at a woman is like a fly sucking on blood.
>
> Let your wife see your wealth but do not trust her with it.
>
> Do not open your heart to your wife, as what you may say to her in private will be repeated in the street.

One husband had a problem - he was haunted by his dead wife and so he spoke to her with a spell:

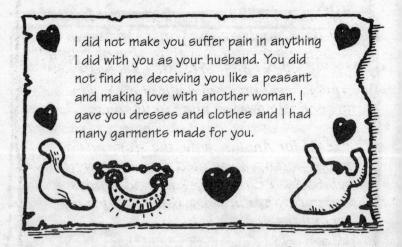

> I did not make you suffer pain in anything I did with you as your husband. You did not find me deceiving you like a peasant and making love with another woman. I gave you dresses and clothes and I had many garments made for you.

Tale Of Two Brothers

Anubis and his brother, Bata, worked on a farm together. Unfortunately Anubis' wife fell in love with Bata. One day when Bata came home from the fields early, she declared her love to him, but he refused her and went back to work. She got frightened that he would tell Anubis, so she covered herself in fat and grease to make it appear she had been beaten. When Anubis came home that evening she lay down pretending to be ill. She did not pour water for his hands in the usual way and she didn't light a fire for him. She told Anubis that Bata had tried to attack her.

Anubis got mad and decided to kill Bata, but Bata managed to escape. And when Anubis came after him Bata was able to tell his brother what had really happened. So Anubis went home and killed his wife instead. He fed her body to the dogs.

Except for Anubis' wife, the story has a happy ending. Bata died and was magically reborn as a Pharaoh's son, and Anubis became Pharaoh when Bata died for the second time.

Divorce Egyptian Style

If things really got out of hand, men and women could divorce. They divided up the property and the one who did not own the house had to go back to his or her parents. First a partner had to prove the other was unsatisfactory, a common complaint was that one or the other was not able to have children.

One-eyed wife

Things could turn nasty. One man had been married for 20 years when he fell in love with another woman. He then rounded on his wife and told her: "I repudiate you because you have no sight in one eye." His wife then scolded him because in 20 years he had never complained before!

BATHS AND BODY ODOUR

LOOKING GOOD AND KEEPING CLEAN

There's no way of knowing, but it's likely that life in Ancient Egypt was pretty smelly and unhealthy at times. There were no chimneys in the houses (air holes in the kitchen roof let smoke escape), the towns were crowded, the sanitation was awful and it got very hot:

Rats and mice must have been common - if they didn't get eaten by the thousands of Ancient Egyptian cats.

Animals would have carried fleas and the fleas could have brought diseases.

Rubbish was either dumped in a local dump, in the river or a canal.

The river Nile acted as the general sewer for the whole country, as well as providing cooking, washing and drinking water.

ANIMAL CRACKERS

The Egyptians were mad about animals, which must have added to the smells. They kept pets such as dogs, monkeys, baboons, cats and even geese. Dogs had names like "Big", "Black" or "Ebony".

Herodotus, a Greek historian, thought the Egyptians were cat crazy. If a house caught on fire, he said they would rescue the cat rather than try to put the fire out. If a pet cat died, they would sometimes shave their eyebrows in mourning.

Sacred animals, like cats and ibis birds, were often given a full burial service. They were preserved as mummies as a matter of course.

Sweet-smelling spices were in demand to cover up the smells. There were other potions to stop insects and other bugs....

Here are some horrible household tips:

 To get rid of fleas: sprinkle the house with natron water.

 To keep mice away: spread cat fat on everything.

 To keep flies way: spread fat from the oriole bird.

To keep a snake in its hole: put an onion by the hole.

WHITER THAN WHITE

Despite the lack of good sewers, Egyptians were not filthy dirty. In fact they were famous for being clean. Herodotus thought they were obsessed with cleanliness as well as animals.

Most Egyptians washed themselves with ashes, natron and soda, which didn't lather and could be scratchy. For a bath they had the river or a canal. Rich people had en-suite limestone bathrooms. They might even have a shower.

CURE FOR BODY ODOUR:

Take some ostrich egg, shell of tortoise and tamarisk nuts, and roast them together, then smear them on the bits that smell.

 Natron is hydrated sodium carbonate. Modern soaps also contain sodium in a different form.

After washing the Egyptians were in the habit of smearing oils on their skin, to stop the skin getting too dry from all the sand and the natron soap. Pregnant women believed oils would help them to avoid marks being left after their skin had stretched while they were pregnant.

Evidently the ultra-rich used a lot of cleansing substances - all the tax from all the fisherman in one Egyptian lake was earmarked to pay for the toiletries of the Queens of Egypt. Queen Cleopatra used to bathe in milk.

They cleaned their teeth with a twig or reed using toothpaste made from roots. People were advised to chew herbs or spices to improve the breath - probably because they ate loads of garlic, onion and radishes.
The rich wore sparkling white clothes. Their dirty linen was collected by the laundryman and returned clean, dry, ironed and re-pleated. Being a laundryman was a busy trade, and it got easier when they learned to give the clothes a hot wash by heating large jars of water by the river bank.

Most people could not afford to use the services of a laundryman. For the women in these families washing was a big chore. Garments were piled into baskets on washday and carried to the edge of the river or canal. The washing went like this:

1. Roll clothes in a ball.

2. Soak them well.

3. Rub with natron soap.

4. Pound with a paddle.

5. Rinse to remove natron.

6. Dry in the sun.

SANITARY TOWEL FIRST

The Egyptians had sanitary towels which they called "bands of the behind". Used ones were sent to the laundry so they could be used again.

TOILET SEAT FIRST

The first known toilet seats were found in the new town of Akhetaten, which was built around 1350 BC. The seats were made of clay, wood or stone, and a large bowl of sand was placed beneath the central hole. Toilet seats were sometimes left in the royal tombs, in case the Pharaoh got caught short.

What A Stink

Animals must have caused problems for Ancient Egyptians – just like nowadays.

DRUNK AS A SKUNK

A Frenzy Of Feasting

There was nothing an Ancient Egyptian liked better than a glass of beer, unless it was another glass of beer. One Pharaoh called Amosis was said to have got sloshed rather than get on with his work as King. A scribe wrote:

> Lend a hand to an elder drunk on beer; respect him as his children should.

Beer was made and drunk by women as well as men, even for breakfast. They could choose from over seventeen brands, plus import labels from Syria and Nubia. The beer was sweet, thick and non-fizzy. It often had to be strained because it was lumpy, and then sipped through a straw.

But you could have one sip too many: "Do not indulge in drinking beer lest you utter evil speech and don't know what you are saying." And the hangover was known in Ancient Egypt: "Yesterday's drunkenness will not quench today's thirst."

Beer was easy to make:

1) Crumble a lightly baked loaf in a jar.

2) Add flour and a little beer to get it started then leave to ferment.

3) After this stage the beer is so lumpy it must be stirred and sieved.

4) Jars were usually stoppered with a leaf and a lump of mud.

Wine was also drunk by both men and women. Sometimes people had to be carried home from drinking parties. There are pictures of women being sick. On one tomb, the lady says: "Give me eighteen cups of wine. I want to drink until I am drunk. My throat is as dry as a straw."

We know a lot about Ancient Egyptian food, because they put meals in the tombs of the dead. The dead didn't eat them and some of these meals have survived to this day. In fact the meals are often in a better state than the mummified bodies.

POSH NOSH

The rich ate well. One picture of a Pharaoh's table shows nineteen different kinds of bread and cakes, seven kinds of beer, two wines, ten different cuts of beef, four kinds of fowl, seven kinds of fruit, plus wheat and barley. Onions are the only vegetable.

For large banquets, animals were slaughtered just before meals as there was no way of preserving meat.

At the end of a meal, a servant would show the guests a small model of a mummy and say : "Drink and be merry for when you die you will be just like this." Dead encouraging!

THIS IS FOR YOU MADAME.

OOH THANKS- DEAD NICE

WAXING LYRICAL

Rich Egyptians knew how to have a good time. Party guests were greeted by serving girls who presented them with garlands of exotic flowers.

Guests were given heavily perfumed wax cones to be worn on the head. The cone would melt during the evening and run down the face - and the wax would be cooling and sweet-smelling. From time to time, a servant girl would come round and top up your cone.

At slap-up feasts, guests would sometimes inhale the scent of the mandrake root in order to "see things".

Revellers were entertained by girl dancers, acrobats and musicians. The dancers were often half nude with lots of make-up. We even know the names of two of them - Hekenu and Iti, a star performing duo.

One Egyptian song went:

Follow your heart and happiness,
Do the things on earth that your heart commands,
Make holiday,
Do not weary of it,
Lo, none is allowed to take his goods with him,
Lo, no one who departs comes back again.

Whoever wrote this song doesn't seem to have been too convinced by the Egyptian beliefs about the after-life – as taking their goods with them was exactly what most Egyptians liked to do!

MEANWHILE...

Things were worse for the poor, even though there seems to have been enough for them to eat most of the time. Breakfast was a small meal. The main meal was at noon, when it was too hot to go outside, and then there was a small supper in the evening.

Breakfast

A day's food for one family might be ten loaves of bread and two jugs of beer, with a few vegetables, perhaps onions, lettuce or radishes, to add a little flavour. With luck there might be some fish or game and they might keep animals for milk, cheese and eggs. Egyptians liked to eat their food plain and much of it was boiled. All in all, it was a very healthy diet, just the thing food experts recommend today.

Egyptian teeth were easily ground down by the gritty flour which bread was made of, and by the fine desert sand, which got everywhere. But they never used sugar, except in the form of date and honey cake, so they didn't have much tooth decay. Some mummies have tooth fillings made from a cement of gum and stone. Others have gold wire to bind loose teeth to strong ones.

BAD MANNERS

Have you got disgusting table manners? If you have, you would not have been welcome at an Egyptian feast. They took their table manners seriously, especially if dining with an important person. Here's some advice:

Don't speak to him unless he speaks to you -you don't know what may displease him. Speak only when he has addressed you, then your words will please his heart.

It wasn't done to pig out on all the lovely food. Here's some more advice:

When you sit down to eat in company, shun the food you love. Restraint only needs a moment's effort, whereas gluttony is base and is reproved.

On the other hand, it seems that it was rude not to eat enough:

'Vile is he whose belly still hungers when the meal time has passed'

JUST A LITTLE CRUMB – PLEASE!

And finally, remember not to hog the best dishes, and to pass things without being asked:

Do not eat bread while another stands by, without offering your portion to him. Food is always here. It is man who does not last.

REALLY – I'M NOT HUNGRY. DO TAKE IT

NO REALLY – I CAN'T.

The menu at one Egyptian feast went like this:

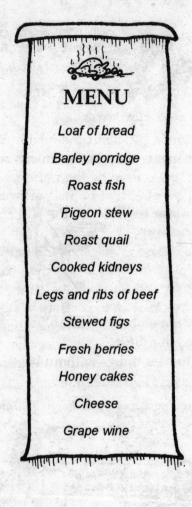

MENU

Loaf of bread

Barley porridge

Roast fish

Pigeon stew

Roast quail

Cooked kidneys

Legs and ribs of beef

Stewed figs

Fresh berries

Honey cakes

Cheese

Grape wine

MUMMY!

(AGAIN)

WRAP ARTISTS AND MAGIC TRICKS

BUT FIRST — SOME SICK NOTES

We know quite a bit about the health of the Ancient Egyptians, because they left so many bodies behind. For instance, by examining the mummy of Ramses II, archaeologists know that he had arthritis of the hip, heart disease and abscesses in the jaw.

People suffered from many of the same diseases as they do today and at least the Egyptians had good doctors by the standards of the time. Their doctors gained a lot of practical experience dissecting animals for sacrifice, and they knew what the inside of the human body looked like, because they could watch the removal of the insides from the dead when they were being made into mummies.

Egyptian doctors used to stitch deep cuts and they could fix broken bones with splints and bandages. They had surgical implements and a doctor's bag for carrying them. They even knew the importance of rest and hygiene for good health.

The doctors also knew a lot about herbal medicine and passed on much of their knowledge to the Greeks. They gave out prescribed medicines in little labelled containers, just like today.

ALL WRAPPED UP AND READY TO GO

People died eventually of course, however good the doctors. Although considering the amount of fuss they made about it, it's hard not to think that the Ancient Egyptians actually looked forward to dying.

They believed that everyone had two souls called Ka and Ba. Preserving the body of someone who had died was a very sensible thing to do because Ka, the life-force of the soul, stayed attached to the body even when it was dead. Ba, the personality, could fly about but had to be able to return to the body. That is why it was so important to preserve dead bodies. No corpse, no Ka and no place for Ba to fly back to.

Ooh mummy!

In the earliest days, the Egyptians tried to preserve the bodies of the dead by burying them in sand. This worked pretty well, because the hot sand dried the body out before it had time to decay.

When more elaborate brick tombs were built, the bodies started to rot because they were no longer kept in dry, hot sand. So they wrapped the body in bandages soaked in resin and painted the face of the dead person on the outer wrappings. These were the first mummies.

At first only top people got this treatment, but gradually it became more popular among the well off. In the end there was a huge mummy industry and millions of people and animals were mummified.

Mummies were once taken as medicine!

The word "mummy" comes from the Persian word "mummia" which means bitumen. (Nowadays used as tar for making roads). Bitumen looks very like the resin used by the Egyptians to preserve bodies, and bitumen was used as a medicine in the Middle East for many years. In the Middle Ages and later, mummies were boiled until the flesh fell off. The bitumen-like preserving resin floated to the surface of the boiling water and hardened as it cooled.

Mummy became a popular and expensive medicine.

RAISED FROM THE DEAD

When they found the mummy of Ramses I, something odd happened. The mummy was left lying out in the sun so long that the resins (gum) grew warm and melted. As the resins melted the body lost some of its stiffness and the king's arm rose into the air - and terrified the workmen.

FIVE GRAVE FACTS

1. In Victorian times, surgeons gave public displays of unwrapping mummies, sometimes using hammer and chisel to do it.

2. One sharp dealer sold the body of an Italian doctor to a keen English mummy-collector, pretending it was a specially well-preserved Egyptian mummy. The collector had it shipped to England.

3. When examining the early tombs, explorers were amazed to find Egyptian fingerprints still preserved on the coffins. The finger-prints of one mummy are even on file at Scotland Yard.

4. Millions of animals were mummified and buried as a mark of respect to their gods. Four million mummified ibis birds, each placed in a pot, were discovered at Saqqara.

5. Around 1900, about 300,000 cat mummies were sent to Liverpool by ship, to be ground up as fertiliser.

HOW TO MAKE A MUMMY:

1. Find a dead body and wash it.

2. Take out the internal organs – heart, lungs, liver and guts. This is because they will rot away if left inside your mummy. Put all the bits and pieces, except for the heart, in separate jars.

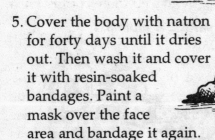

3. Mash the brain up inside the head with a long, thin hook and then drain it out through the left nostril.

4. Put the heart back in the body. One theory was that the heart would be weighed on the scales of truth.

5. Cover the body with natron for forty days until it dries out. Then wash it and cover it with resin-soaked bandages. Paint a mask over the face area and bandage it again.

6. Your mummy is ready for burial!

PREPARING FOR THE OFF

After a body had been mummified it was put in its coffin. But first it was vitally necessary to perform the *Opening of the Mouth* ceremony. The front leg of a bull was pointed at it, and the face was touched by special objects. This made sure that the body would "come

back to life" so that the dead person would be able to breathe and live in the next world.

Then before the whole coffin was sealed, the mummy was given a copy of *The Book of the Dead*. This was a kind of handbook of magic charms and handy hints for getting to the next world.

Important mummies might go into three coffins, each fitting inside the other like Russian dolls. They were crawling inside and out with magic writing and pictures. The eyes of the falcon-headed god Horus were painted on the outside so that the mummy could see out of the coffin. Helpful as always, the coffin makers painted a tiny false door so that the Ba could leave.

Now the body was ready for burial.

For a mighty Pharaoh, the funeral procession would cross the river from Thebes on the east bank of the Nile, otherwise known as the land of the living. Once on the west side they would pick up the body which would already have crossed the river to be mummified in the funerary workshops. The west side was called the land of the dead.

When a funeral procession had collected a mummy, the body was placed in a booth which was decked with flowers then mounted on a boat-shaped frame, or bier. This contraption was pulled on a sled by oxen. A priest walked at the front of the procession, sprinkling milk and swinging a censer. He was followed by the most important guests. The wife or husband sat beside the bier and the mummy was attended by two women mourners, representing the goddesses Isis and Nephthys, who had mourned for Osiris.

No funeral was complete without a bunch of women wailers dressed in blue. These professional mourners were paid to wail and scream and tear their hair. The rest of the women (relatives and suchlike) dressed in white or blue-grey linen and followed the procession, also making a great show of grief – loud wailing, beating bare breasts, smearing the body with dirt and tearing at dishevelled hair.

After the women came a long stream of servants carrying bags and baggage, furniture, clothing, jewellery, food, flowers, wine, and models of people, buildings and boats – everything you might need if you were going abroad for a few years. They didn't take the kitchen sink, but they did take portable toilets sometimes.

Poor people were buried simply, often in cheap wooden coffins, but even the poor often managed to take some small personal goods with them, such as pots, headrests and jewellery.

BA HAD THE BODY OF A BIRD

THE LAST JOURNEY

At last with the body safely tucked up in its tomb, it was safe for the Ba soul to complete its last, dangerous journey which had begun at the funeral service.

With Ka, the life-force, safely protecting the mummy, perhaps also protected by the magic of the priests, Ba was ready to make its glorious dash for the Field of Reeds and to enter the Kingdom of Osiris.

It was a dangerous journey through the underworld. Ba might be attacked by serpents, crocodiles and other monsters which lay in wait. Finally it would be weighed in a pair of scales against the Feather of Truth. Only if it was lighter could it go to the Field of Reeds and live in happiness for ever.

ARE THEY STILL THERE?

EGYPT AFTER THE PHARAOHS

The descendants of the Ancient Egyptians still live beside the river Nile. But although their descendants are alive, the ancient language and religion are as dead as the thousands of dry sheets of ancient Egyptian papyrus which moulder in museums across the world. The great Egyptian civilization is over and finished. For nearly 2,000 years no further bodies have been mummified. The priests and the Pharaohs have gone, and only the massive remains of the temples and

pyramids shimmer in the desert heat, like vast empty houses, to remind us of the hopes and dreams of the amazing Ancient Egyptians who lived so long ago.

Who knows what has happened to all the Ba souls which once made it to the Kingdom of Osiris, and which they made such huge efforts to protect, now that their mummies have been dug up and their tombs have been pilfered?

Are they still there?..

A PLATE OF DATES

A FEW DATES TO CHEW ON...

Ever eaten Egyptian dates? Here's a packet for you. The dates are a bit rough; Ancient Egypt happened such an incredibly long time ago that no one can be entirely sure of exact dates .

PRE-DYNASTIC PERIOD, up to 3100 BC
Stone age people slowly develop Egyptian farming to form the Kingdoms of Upper and Lower Egypt. Flat-top mastaba tombs built at Sakkara and Abydos.

EARLY DYNASTIC, 3100-2680 BC, Dynasties 1-2
Union of the two Egypts under Menes, with capital at Memphis. Large-scale irrigation introduced.

> Turn over for more Dynastic dates

Generally, it's useful to think in threes. Three kingdoms. Three thousand years of recorded history. Thirty dynasties.

Old kingdom

2680-2180 BC, Dynasties 3-6
The great age of pyramids. Wars with Libya and Nubia.

1ST INTERMEDIATE, 2180-2050 BC, Dynasties 7-10
Civil war between the north and south. North and south separated again.

Middle kingdom

2050-1780 BC, Dynasties 11-13
Egypt re-united with capital at Thebes, where the god Amun is worshipped. Nubia is conquered.

2ND INTERMEDIATE, 1780-1560 BC, Dynasties 14-17
The Hyksos invaders from Asia take over Lower Egypt and the Nubians separate from Upper Egypt.

1560-1085 BC, Dynasties 18-20

Pharaoh Ahmose expels the Hyksos. The Egyptian empire spreads to Nubia in the south and to the Euphrates in the north-east. Thebes becomes the capital city. Temples are built at Abydos, Abu Simbel and Karnak. Libyan and Sea People are repelled but Egyptian power declines. Egypt divided again and Nubia lost.

3RD INTERMEDIATE, 1085-716 BC, Dynasties 21-24

Egypt divided, with Libyans ruling the north.

LATE PERIOD, 716-333 BC, Dynasties 25-30

Invasions by Nubians, Assyrians, Persians (twice). Finally conquered by Greeks under Alexander the Great, and under Queen Cleopatra Greek Egypt becomes a Roman province.

GRAND SAND QUIZ

Now that you've finished the book, try my Quiz to test your Egyptian expertise. Answers on page 125.

SECTION 1 – DISCOVERING ANCIENT EGYPT

1) Why did Napolean invade Egypt?

a) To search for buried treasure?

b) To stop the British going to India and to get a colony for himself?

c) Because he'd gone completely mad?

2) What was the Rosetta stone?

a) A famous ancient Egyptian stone-carving of a flower?

b) The doorway to a secret tomb?

c) An ancient tablet with Greek and Egyptian writing on it?

SECTION 2 – ANCIENT EGYPTIAN LEARNING

3) What is a hieroglyph?

a) A heraldic lion?

b) A picture letter?

c) Napolean's coat-of-arms?

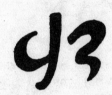

4) What did Egyptian scribes write on in scribe-school?

a) Paper made from cotton or wood?

b) Pottery or limestone?

c) The walls of pyramids?

5) What was a cubit?

a) A small box?

b) A type of sweet?

c) A measurement of length?

SECTION 3 – ANCIENT EGYPTIAN LIFESTYLES

5) What was the ancient Egyptian award for bravery?

a)The Golden Mouse?

b) A curved sword?

c) The Golden Fly?

6) What was the first ball game?

a) Pharonic football??

b) A kind of cricket?

c) Temple tennis?

7) What was the Egyptians'
   favourite pet?

a) Baboons

b) Cows

c) Cats

8) What was the most massive
   building of ancient Egypt?

a) The step pyramid at Meidum?

b) The Great Pyramid at Giza?

c) The Great Temple of Karnak?

SECTION 4 – DEATH, THE EGYPTIAN WAY

9) Why did Egyptians have themselves
mummified after death?

a) So that people centuries later would have someting
   to wonder about?

b) Because they believed that they could only enjoy
   the spiritual afterlife if their body was preserved
   on earth?

c) So that relatives could visit their departed loved
   ones years after they'd died?

10) What did Seth do to Osiris?

a) He worshipped him?

b) He fell in love with his wife?

c) He tore him into little pieces?

11) What happened to Tutankhamen's trumpet?

a) It was stolen by grave-robbers.

b) It was as silent as the curse of Osiris.

c) It was blown again after 3,000 years.

ANSWERS TO GRAND SAND QUIZ

1) b. see page 10

2) c. see page 11

3) b. see page 12

4) b. see pages 57, 58

5) c. see page 72

6) b. see page 45

7) c. see pages 76, 79, 94-95,

8) b. see pages 26, 28, 50

9) b. see page 108

10) c. see page 48

11) c. see page 33

If you scored more than fifty (10 points for each correct answer) consider yourself an Egyptian expert. If you got less than fifty – it's back to scribe-school for you!

ANSWER TO PUZZLE ON PAGE 13:

The message reads 'beneath tree'.

INDEX

READ ON

More books to read on Ancient Egypt.

ANCIENT EGYPT by Anne Millard
Usborne Pocket Guides
This is a tiny book full of drawings and brief descriptions which gives you a really quick time trip back to the Pharaohs.

ANCIENT EGYPT
Dorling Kindersley pocket book series
Packed with photographs and brief commentaries.

THE EGYPTIAN WORLD by Margaret Oliphant
Kingfisher History Library
A good book with a large format, clear illustrations and good explanations about living in Egypt.

ANCIENT EGYPT
Dorling Kindersley Eyewitness guide
This book was produced in association with the British Museum where there are loads of Egyptian mummies and other spooky stuff.

THE SEARCH FOR ANCIENT EGYPT
Thames and Hudson - New Horizon series
This books is about Egyptologists - the people who rediscovered Egypt.